MINIMALIST BUDGET

Grow Your Dough, Budgeting Like a Pro! Minimalism Money Management, Personal Finance & Investing Basics For Beginners!

JASON DELUCCI

© Copyright 2019 – (Jason Delucci) All rights reserved.

The contents of this book may not be reproduced, duplicated or transmitted without direct written permission from the author. Under no circumstances will any legal responsibility or blame be held against the publisher for any reparation, damages, or monetary loss due to the information herein, either directly or indirectly.

Legal Notice:

This book is copyright protected. This is only for personal use. You cannot amend, distribute, sell, use, quote or paraphrase any part or the content within this book without the consent of the author.

Disclaimer Notice:

Please note the information contained within this document is for educational and entertainment purposes only. Every attempt has been made to provide accurate, up to date and reliable complete information. No warranties of any kind are expressed or implied. Readers acknowledge that the author is not engaging in the rendering of legal, financial, medical or professional advice. The content of this book has been derived from various sources. Please consult a licensed professional before attempting any techniques outlined in this book.

By reading this document, the reader agrees that under no circumstances are is the author responsible for any losses, direct or indirect, which are incurred as a result of the use of information contained within this document, including, but not limited to, —errors, omissions, or inaccuracies.

TABLE OF CONTENTS

Introduction 1
   Old School Thinking 3
   Why I'm Writing This Book 5

Part 1: Plugging the Holes 7

Chapter 1: Back to Basics Budgeting 9
   Getting Real 10
   Making an Inventory 11
   A Word on Taxes 14

Chapter 2: Stopping the Bleeding 15
   Making Sacrifices 15
   Simplified Spending 17
   Fixed vs Flexible Expenses 19
   Consolidate Banking and Credit Cards 21

Chapter 3: Good Debt vs Bad Debt 23
   The Good, Bad & In-Between 24
   Debt Clearing Strategy 28
   Assets Vs Liabilities 29
   Renting Vs Buying 30

Part 2: Filling the Bucket 33

Chapter 4: Growing Wealth the Right Way 35
   Cash Flow Will Always Be King 36
   What They Don't Teach You at School 38
   Traditional Allocation Rules 39
   Your Personal Economic Ecosystem 40

Chapter 5: Growth Curves & Money Projections. 47
   Parkinson's Law 47
   Compounding Interest 49
   Pareto Principle 50

Chapter 6: Delaying Gratification 55
   Short Term Goals = Long Term Payoffs 55
   Thinking in Probabilities 56
   Marshmallows & Money 58
   Summary: Saving Dollars, Making Cents… 61
   Core Concepts Summary 61
   A Crisis is Always in the Making 63
   Conclusion 67

Bonus Chapter 69

Chapter 6: Transportation & Travel 71
   Transit Tips 71
   Vacation Considerations 73

INTRODUCTION

So there I was standing in front of the ATM at my local 7-Eleven. There was a line of hurried people standing behind me. But no matter how long I stared at the screen, I still only had $18 in my student checking account. In fact, it wasn't even my $18. I was $982 overdrawn so was fast approaching my $1000 credit limit. I wasn't sure that you could withdraw any less than $20? I'll try $10. Bingo! It worked. A six-inch subway for lunch it was then…

My financial predicament may not have seemed too drastic to some people, but I assure you, to that 23-year-old just out of college, it wasn't ideal. Not only did I have next to nothing in liquid cash to survive, but I also had a little over $30k in student loans to pay back at some point. Fortunately, I had the rest of my 20's to sort it out, or so I thought. I proceeded to be loose with my money. I bought a pair shiny new sneakers every few months and could never so no to those expensive weekend trips away. In truth, all of this was a desperate attempt to put off responsible adult life for a little while longer.

One day I decided that this couldn't continue. It was time to sort this mess out once and for all. So I stopped all unnecessary spending and got myself that stable job my parents were always hounding me to get. However, it wasn't long before I began making the second major monetary mistake of my budding financial career. I got myself that way too expensive apartment and least cost efficient car I thought I could afford (I did love that BMW 5 series why the fun lasted).

But it didn't take long before the music stopped and my exuberant lifestyle experiment blew up in the midst of the 2008 financial crisis. I've described this period in greater depth in other editions within this minimalism series, so I'll save you the explanation again here. All I say is that it taught me a precious lesson — one which prompted me to try this minimalism thing out in the first place. Combined with a major move to a different country, my outlook on life began to change radically.

I'm not suggesting you go back-packing around the world in order to escape your financial troubles. That will almost certainly make things worse. Taking responsibility for your situation is the first rule of sound budgeting. But often changing your physical location and surroundings can serve as the psychological nudge you need to alter your thinking.

That's because many of the strategies required to really get your finances in order can seem quite drastic, to begin with. Although after some practice they'll seem subtle and you'll forget what it was like to function in the old way of doing things. As I say, it takes a mindset shift in the beginning, much like minimalism in general. So stick with me as I'll show you how to ease into them, which is especially relevant if you're an older individual with more liabilities. If you're younger with fewer financial burdens, then its a lot easier so there's no excuse to not get these principles rolling immediately.

I was fortunate enough to learn this lesson quite early on. Not early enough for my liking but certainly in time to start improving my life considerably when I reached my early thirties. My aim isn't to make you feel depressed about your current situation whatever stage of life you might be at, as in truth, starting these prudent financial practices is a wise thing to do at any point in time. You just have the added benefit of extra years or even decades to compound these good habits if you catch them early enough.

Money is a funny thing, as it has so many psychological connotations connected to it. Fear, stress, and worry for a start, especially when we have a lack of it. We literally feel like our very survival is pegged to the number we see when logging into our online statements. On the flip side, we feel joy, comfort, and peace of mind when we do have some extra shekels. It's so freeing when you no longer have to look at the price tags when buying things. I'm not talking about being rash with your spending. But simply being able to go to the grocery store to buy your family everything they need without worrying about the cost.

Old School Thinking

Most people think of budgeting as boring behavior. They perceive it as a drab mechanism of spending less, saving more and rationing 1940's style with what they do have. It's viewed as a draconian austerity measure which sucks the fun out of life. Much like minimalism in general, they equate budgeting with a scarcity mentality. They see it as a restrictive exercise where they will have to start going without. I'm here to tell you that's not the case. I want you to get out of this old school mindset. While its a stretch to claim that minimalist budgeting is sexy, it's certainly more appealing when you look at it from a growth standpoint. You might not like the process at first, but when you start to see your accounts going from red to black, it becomes a lot more fun I promise you.

In essence, what I'm suggesting just follows the minimalist principles stated in my previous books. What we are talking about here is condensing and simplifying your finances in the same way — reducing things to only what works — not making the process needlessly confusing and convoluted as most accountants would have you believe. Eliminating waste leaving only the critical is the best way to ensure success in anything, not least with your personal finances. Growing and retaining wealth is achieved by implementing just a few simple concepts and sticking to them. It's not rocket science, but it's effective. It's not about performing complicated accounting gymnastics with your day-to-day spending habits, but rather sticking to a predetermined playbook which ensures success.

In this sense, this book isn't about money per se, but rather a lifestyle. It's about making a mental shift in your outlook and subsequent behaviors which will have the best payoff for you in the long term. Money isn't everything, but its the only thing people keep track of. It's important to achieve stability in life, so you might as well learn how to make this work for you. Get your finances right, and you can enjoy a life of complete and utter joy and harmony.

Why I'm Writing This Book

Managing your personal finances is a skill like any other. But one they do not teach you in school. Its the number one topic people tell me they wished they had learned at an earlier age. It's not that they want mountains of money to dive into each weekend like Scrooge McDuck (kudos to those old enough to remember that cartoon). They simply want freedom. They want to be free from the feelings of anxiety, worry and stress that having a lack of financial security brings. They just want peace of mind that they can pay the bills and put food on the table each month. This is eminently possible with just a little planning, regardless of your overall income. It's a machine you can plug into which will alleviate these negative feelings before long. In fact, these simple concepts will grow a persons confidence like nothing else I've seen.

Whether you like it or not, the middle class are continually getting squeezed across the world. Around 80% of American households have less than a year's salary in savings. This is especially frightening when you realize that approximately 100 million of these people have no retirement vehicles to fall back on in terms of pensions or 401(k)s. It's pretty clear the dire state we are getting ourselves into, and the only person who can sort it out is you: not your parents, spouse, your church and least of all your government.

So don't skim over these concepts or take them lightly. Material like this is meant to be implemented, not merely consumed. I've laid out each chapter in a specific way, so one concept builds on the next. Taking action on these steps is the only way to ensure you begin making tangible progress in your own circumstances. Once you get the basics right, everything will fall into place that much easier. Your financial life will just seem to now run on autopilot as if by magic. But not without a little effort and planning first.

This is the final piece of the puzzle within this minimalist story. Reducing the clutter in your house and mind is one thing. Getting your finances in order is the icing on the cake to living a genuinely freeing minimalist existence. So let's waste no more time discussing the benefits on proper budgeting and money management, let me show you how it's done.

PART 1: PLUGGING THE HOLES

CHAPTER 1: BACK TO BASICS BUDGETING

"A budget is telling your money where to go instead of wondering where it went"

(John Maxwell)

Many people complain about a "cookie cutter" approach when it comes to budgeting. They say things like "I'm different, I have such and such to deal with which means I can't budget my money like everyone else." The thing is, they're right. We all have different circumstances, mouths to feed, bills to pay, etc. But that is just a cop-out in my experience. These excuses give people the license to get away with spending what they want to spend. It provides flexibility where it's not needed.

But like anything worthwhile you are grappling with, managing your finances takes discipline. I can tell you what you want to hear or I can tell you what works. But people want their cake and to eat it too. Don't get me wrong; this won't seem restrictive in the least once you get used to it. But there are some overriding principles which everyone has to stick to starting out. They are tried and tested formulas I've come across which have not only worked wonders for me but countless others I've recommended them to over the years. I'll be highlighting precisely what these are as we go.

Getting Real

Most people also do not want to look at their finances when they know they aren't in great shape. This is understandable, and I've been there believe me. They put off opening their statements as they are scared of what they will find. Afraid of just how much they are paying in interest on that 18% APR credit card. But this is the first thing you need to rectify. No matter how bad you perceive your current money situation to be, you must own up to it and get clear with every detail.

Money is like anything else, its a habit you have to get used to handling. You have to get the inflows and outflows under control, not continue to stay blind to them. Any issues you might have, cease to be a problem if you genuinely assess the situation and come up with a legitimate game plan to fix things and get ahead of them. That's where this book comes in. So you can finally take hold of the reins of your financial destiny, which means your entire destiny, as everything in this world is linked to your economic status whether we like it or not.

So let's take the first steps on this journey. Yes, the calculations will differ slightly from month to month. Vacation season in July/August may cost you a little more, as will festive season in November/December. But it starts with mapping out your finances to get a granular view on exactly what's going on.

Making an Inventory

First things first, you have to list out EVERY outlay and income you have. You have to track all expenses large and small. This is best done on a simple spreadsheet or Google document in my experience. But if you want to get a little fancier, there are plenty of online budgeting tools such as Mint.com. Just take a look to see which one best suits your style, but ensure you stick to the following criteria whichever tracking method you choose.

Category 1

Incoming = Salary (Job), Business Income (Online/Physical Store), Investments/Capital Gains (Appreciation/Dividends from a Stock Portfolio, House Rental Income, etc)

Category 2

Outgoings = Housing (Mortgage/Rent), Utilities (Phone, Internet, Electricity, Water Bills), Food (Groceries, Dining Out), Transportation (Car, Bus/Train Passes), Clothing, Childcare, Gym, Entertainment (Cinema, Drinking, Trips), Any miscellaneous (Gifts, Car Repairs, Emergencies etc).

As an example, let's take the average median annual income of an America household today (2018) which is a little over $59,000. That is $4916 per month. Lets round that figure up t0 $5000 per month to make the maths a little cleaner. So we have as follows:

Category 1

Incoming (per month) = $5000 (Salary), $500 (Stock Dividends)

Total = $5500

Category 2

Outgoing (per month) = $2000 (Rent), $500 (Car), $300 (Car Insurance), $200 (Gas), $200 (Utilities), $400 (Food), $300 (Entertainment), $50 (Gym), $50 (Miscellaneous).

Total = $4000

This scenario produces a positive cash flow of $1500, I.e., the difference between the net income and outgoings when the latter is subtracted from the former. This is the key to everything we'll discuss within this book and personal finance in general. It's absolutely imperative that you can produce this financial buffer between what is coming into your bank accounts and what is going out each month. I know this somewhat oversimplified advice, but it's the only way you can start to rectify any bad debt situations and create a positive accumulation scenario instead. It underpins all of the subsequent philosophies we will lay out both technically and psychologically.

You will have two options when it comes to creating this positive balance, the first being growing top line income (which we'll discuss further in Part 2). This takes some time and obviously more work. So the easier thing you can do in the meantime is cut expenditure to reduce outgoings. The magic happens when you can do both simultaneously. But let's start by getting crystal clear with your current financial's and start to see where we can make some adjustments to rectify any obvious bleeding. To see where the major leaks are in your system.

You have to do this significant overhaul once. Then set a definite day/date when you will assess this inflow/outflow every month. I do it on the 4th so I can clearly see all expenses and income that have come and gone in the prior month. Staying on top of these things is a new habit you MUST cultivate. You have to keep your finger on your financial pulse at all times. You have to treat your money like a mischievous toddler, to begin with. Keep a close eye on it to track its movements and more importantly, know when anything is getting out of hand.

A minimalist approach to budgeting just means keeping things as simple as possible to help you with this. You don't need to have sky-high financial literacy or a business and accounting MBA, just the basic knowledge of how money works. Some common sense understanding and again, exactly how your individual finances are flowing. This is easier if you have consistent incomings and outgoings which you can more accurately predict on a month-to-month basis. Just do the best you can, to begin with as you will start to get a good feel for how your accounts are working with just a few short months of tracking them.

A Word on Taxes

There is no getting away from the fact that taxes will play a significant role in any discussion when it comes to personal finances and budgeting. However, exploring the ins and outs of taxes is a far broader scope for a book such as this due to the complex nature of this topic. These factors will differ greatly with regards to your type of income I.e. personal, capital gains, etc. But also your location, I.e., country or state in which you live or have domiciled a business.

It's an individuals responsibility to sit down with their accountant and work out what you need to pay and when. But most importantly, how your taxes will affect your take-home bottom line income. All of the examples and working scenarios in this book will presuppose after-tax figures. I understand this will make things much more conservative than people would hope for, especially if you live in a high-income tax region such as California. But you have to do what you can. The overriding principles I lay out simply work when correctly put into place. So just ensure your taxes are inline and fully accounted for when going through your own figures. Ignore them at your peril!

CHAPTER 2: STOPPING THE BLEEDING

"The most important thing to do if you find yourself in a hole, is to stop digging"

(Warren Buffett)

In the previous chapter, we outlined a personal finance example which is actually the best case scenario for many people. Because if truth be told, most folks are upside down in their monthly cash flow calculations, I.e., they have more going out than coming in! Or at the very best they are breaking even, which means also falling behind and still going into debt, albeit a little more slowly. When you account for taxes, the interest they are paying on any loans in addition to the rate of inflation, they are merely treading water and going under just a little more each month.

Making Sacrifices

So how do we go about fixing this? First, lets look at some specific places we can make the easiest inroads with regards to our initial budgeting endeavors. Most people will suggest foregoing that daily Starbucks in favor of your supermarkets home brand instant coffee or cutting out cable TV. They claim that you should be buying the expiring groceries and scanning online websites for the cheapest flight deals. In my experience, this is all sound and prudent advice, and we'll discuss some further ways to make these small savings shortly.

But what makes the most significant difference over time is undoubtedly your big item outlays. If you are scrutinizing your inflow/outflow categories correctly, then you should clearly identify what these are, I.e., your house and vehicle-related payments should be jumping out at you. So the sensible thing to do is to focus on where you can make the biggest impact first or certainly don't make the situation any worse. Put off buying that up-sized house for a few years. Delay upgrading the family car which comes with increased insurance and maintenance costs.

Don't finance yourself up to the eyeballs with these payments like everybody else. If you truly want to get ahead financially, you will have to do what others aren't prepared to do for a while. You may have to make some of these sacrifices in order to achieve your net positive cash flow each month. But its well worth it. That's how you win at this game in the long term. I waited for years until I bought my first house and I won't upgrade my Honda Civic until doing so won't even make a dent in my net cash flow.

In my experience, the two most impactful things you can do for your future financial self is to 1) Grow your overall top line income, and 2) Simultaneously reduce the cost of these more substantial and expensive items. This will significantly cut expenditure and increase bottom line take home income more than anything else. However, I did promise to identify some areas you can make some minor adjustments to your spending and increase savings in the meantime. While some view these as "penny-pinching" measures, there's no doubt that they do add up over time. So if you want to implement these then by all means do.

Simplified Spending

The following are some of the simple spending and saving methods I've found to work well over the years. These will sound like common sense tactics to the average adult, so I won't elaborate on them too much in fear of insulting your intelligence:

Coffee: Buy the instant brands at your local supermarket and make for yourself while at home/in the office. If you have to buy some coffee on the go, try McDonald's or Dunkin' Donuts while on the road. Pro tip; these are some of the highest quality retail coffees you can buy at around 50% of the cost of your average Starbucks. I purchase black coffees for the most part so you fancy cappuccino lovers might need to get a little more creative.

Groceries: It's no secret that I'm a fan of organic produce due to the high nutritional content and low pesticide residues contained within them. But I understand this option is significantly more expensive. If I had to reduce my grocery bill as a short term measure to get my expenses down, I wouldn't have a problem going for the regular bell peppers and broccoli. Yes, they will contain fewer vitamins, minerals, and anti-oxidants compared with the produce in your local Wholefoods outlets. But it's far better than purchasing the low-cost sugary sweets and snacks. Resist the urge to buy these at all costs as they will end up costing you far more in medical bills in the long run. Balancing your budget at the expense of your health can often be the toughest call for people to make.

Clothing: If you are sticking to the main minimalist mantras then you should have significantly cut down your clothing over the past weeks and months. So maintaining a minimalist wardrobe will naturally save you in both storage space and cost. I do suggest upping the quality if you are reducing the quantity of your clothing. But in the short term as a means to an end, by all means, head to H&M to pick up your jeans and T-shirts while you get your finances in check.

Cell Phone/Cable/Internet Plans: Very few people shop around for this stuff as humans are typically very lazy creatures. But if you want to save an extra 5 bucks a month, you will have to do some searching and negotiating with your local technology and digital service providers. It usually just takes a quick phone call to your current company to see what better deal they can offer you. If they can't, then switch to a competitor who will almost always better your current contract in order to secure your long term business.

Transport: I talk about transit tips in much greater detail within *"Minimalist Living."* You have to be performing a cost vs. time analysis on every decision you are making throughout the day (the above examples included). But no more so than with regards to the regular transportation choices you make each day. Taking public transport rather than driving your car is usually the big decision for most people. Just see where you can sensibly make some savings to shave off some transport dollars from your monthly expenses without significantly impacting your day.

This also very much applies to flights. Air travel can get expensive, and it's a good idea to know where to find cheaper tickets. But don't fret over a 5% saving if you have to tack on an extra two days to your trip due to ridiculous connections and layover times. We are minimalists after all and want to make our lives the most efficient possible in all areas, which certainly includes our time. Simply booking way in advance of your travel dates if you can is still the best way to secure the lowest prices.

Fixed vs Flexible Expenses

Continuing the discussion with regards to spending and savings, there is one final consideration you should be making when assessing your outgoings. We need to explore the differences between fixed and flexible expenses more thoroughly, to once more, see where we can make the most apparent reductions. To make your life a little easier it's wise to group your outgoings into the two following categories:

Fixed Expenditure (Mandatory)

- House Payments
- Car Payments
- Utility Bills
- School Fees
- Grocery Shopping
- Agreed upon savings

While these are indeed fixed outgoings for the most part, as I've already stated, it doesn't mean they can't be reduced or negotiated down.

Flexible Expenditure (Discretionary)

- Clothing Costs
- Subscriptions (Netflix, Cable etc)
- Entertainment
- Eating Out
- Travel

These are areas that can quickly be eliminated or significantly reduced by choice. You should be applying the "simplified spending" methods towards all of these activities. If we are not careful we can fall into the compulsive spending and conspicuous consumption habits I've described a length in previous editions in this minimalism series. In essence, buying unnecessary things to signify our social status. Obviously something to be avoided at all costs when attempting to balance the books.

It all comes down to our personal psychology as always. We merely need to adjust our thinking before we can improve our spending habits. Analyzing where we can make savings with regards to these fixed expenses as well of cutting out many of these flexible expenses, can go a long way to helping us achieve this positive cash flow scenario we are striving for.

Consolidate Banking and Credit Cards

A final area to consider is with regards to your banking and credit cards. I'm not saying get rid of cards and accounts that you'll need. That's counterproductive. After all, it's crucial to have separate accounts to segregate business and personal money etc. But don't hold onto credits cards and store cards that you really don't need. It's a pain in the butt when you lose your wallet and have to remember all of the account and security information when canceling them. You also run the risk of fraud and people stealing money from them. If it sounds like I'm paranoid, then it's for a good reason. This happened to me twice in quick succession when first starting out in my working life. I had my wallet stolen from the gym and left it in the back of a cab all in the space of six months.

So do yourself a favor, and consolidate any accounts you can and get rid of any cards you no longer need. Not only will this simplify things dramatically, its another measure to curb any compulsive and unnecessary spending. Like every other area of your life, employing minimalism to clean up your financial accounts is just a great thing to do.

CHAPTER 3: GOOD DEBT VS BAD DEBT

There's no getting away from the fact that we live in a debt culture, we have for some time now. Everywhere you look, we are up to our eyeballs in the stuff. Individuals, companies, and countries have taken on record levels of indebtedness which accelerated considerably following the financial crisis of 2008. We take out personal loans to finance our lifestyles rather than saving for them. Governments sell bonds to fund their spending instead of responsibly managing budgets. This type of behavior is merely mortgaging the future. We are taxing our future selves and yet unborn generations with the burden of paying the interest from what we consume today, but can't afford...

You only have to a glance at the current fiscal figures to get a picture of how extreme this situation has gotten. The average American household now harbors $136,000 of debt. Granted much of this includes low-interest home mortgages. But the rest is comprised of credit cards (circa $6,900), auto loans ($28,000), and student loans coming in at ($47,600). Whatever way you want to square these numbers, it doesn't look good. No wonder there's been a big uptake of minimalism in the past decade or so.

But not all of this debt is bad I hear you cry! Well, let's discuss this a little further to find out. Some people will preach that all debt is bad and that you shouldn't ever take on a penny. I agree with this sentiment in most cases especially when it comes to the typical items we're acquiring it for. But there are certainly a few acceptations to this rule. There are some instances in life where it's OK, even sensible to take on some debt. So how do we differentiate between the two? Let's take a look.

The Good, Bad & In-Between

The Bad: We all know that one person who maxes out their credit cards to buy a new outfit every week just to keep their wardrobe fresh. Or to go on that way too expensive vacation with the family. This is obviously unwise behavior to the everyday thinking person. Because the truth is, anything you are not getting a return on, I.e., clothes, holidays, etc are bad debt decisions. Especially if you are using eye-watering 18%-20% APR credit to buy them. It could be argued that you are gaining the experience and memories from these purchases, but at what cost! My number one rule is that anything which doesn't benefit my future self in some way, I.e., Instant gratification activities, I pay for in cash I've saved. This will include all travel, entertainment, and toys.

In addition to this, I also don't take out finance for anything that is highly depreciating, like a car or motorbike. These items lose obscene amounts of value when driving them off the showroom floor. I'm not suggesting not to buy a car, as they are a necessity for most people, just know how much you are losing on it each year and borrow against it accordingly. There is one exception to this, that being vehicles which are required for business travel or transportation like trucks, etc. These will pay for themselves if used wisely. But for most people, it's far better to run the family Sedan into the ground before purchasing that shiny new SUV to impress the neighbors.

The Good: On the flip side of this, you want to take out finance for anything which is giving me a positive ROI into the future. This is typically cash flowing assets like small businesses and rental properties (more on this shortly). Notice that I didn't say appreciating items, because in my experience its unwise to bank on the continual increase in the value of an asset. Nobody knows what will happen in the future, and re-mortgaging your house every five years to finance your upgraded lifestyle is a terrible idea indeed. Just ask anyone who took out a 120% homeowner loan in 2007…

However, as I mentioned, I do agree with securing sensible loans to grow an existing business which has PROVEN to be profitable. Never borrow money to start a business with no proof of concept or track record. I see start-ups make this mistake all of the time. They attempt to secure rounds of funding and have to give large percentages of the company away in return. Why not try to bootstrap it first? Then once you have a solid foundation to build on and a clear strategy to scale the business, only then is it wise to seek extra finance to take things to the next level. There just needs to be a clear path of dollars in vs. dollars out.

This doesn't include any loans for investing. We also will get onto how to allocate funds for these things from you top line income later on. I see many people make the mistake of borrowing to buy into 4%-7% annual return index tracker stock funds. While the fund average might reflect these numbers over the past 30 years, much like appreciating assets, there's no telling what might happen in the next 5-10 years. This is especially true if you are borrowing at rates of 10-12% to do so. These figures are obviously upside down, and any significant market correction would put you in serious strife.

The In-between: Virtually everyone I meet has no issue with the advice mentioned above regarding good and bad debt. It's just common sense stuff. However, there are some gray areas of controversy. There is no right or wrong answer here necessarily as this will depend on your experiences, skill levels, age, and overall risk tolerance. Your primary residence or home is the best example of this. Depending on the location and how long you plan to live at this place will determine whether a 30-year mortgage is a good idea. I historically preferred to be more mobile, but now I have a small family on the way, I'm considering bunking down in my current abode and buying it out.

Student loans are the second category of debt which splits opinions. I do agree that personal education is an excellent investment to make. But most college courses teach you very little about how to function in today's economy. Gone are the days that having a biology or geography degree would give you an edge in the market place. These folks struggle to attain minimum wage entry-level positions after graduating now. We are quickly migrating back to a skills-based economy. Therefore, its far better to get an apprenticeship now to learn a vocation in a fraction of the time and cost of the average degree. Of course, the exceptions to this would be the aspiring doctors, lawyers, and engineers who require official training at these institutions. But for your average media studies student, I would skip the $30,000 debt and get your foot in the door of a company instead and work your way up.

Credit cards are the final debt tool which can be used for both good and evil purposes. As I've already mentioned, most people use them for awful purchases quite frankly. However, to the established and responsible individual or business owner, credit cards certainly have some upsides when used correctly. By this, I mean only borrowing on them sparingly and paying off the outstanding balance EVERY month. Doing this will help you build your credit rating and raise your overall financial profile. They allow you to accumulate loyalty points, air-miles, but most importantly of all, will enable you to secure better lending rates for the big purchase (like the house and car) later down the line.

Debt Clearing Strategy

We can't have a discussion on budgeting without also considering a strategy to clear any existing debt you may have accumulated over the years. This is especially relevant with regards to any bad debt you have. When people ask me what they should be doing in this instance, I always suggest the following three steps:

1) Stop taking on any more high-interest borrowing (credits/store cards etc.)

2) Switch any existing high-interest loans to 0% balance transfers for the next 12-18 months.

3) Pay off the existing debts in monthly increments starting with the smallest first.

By doing these three things, you will initially arrest the bleeding. You will prevent the situation from getting any worse. Switching to promotional rates with different credit card companies will then give you some breathing space while you are implementing the final step. This being to start making a dent in your existing balances. Most people will tell you to begin paying off the highest interest loan first. This seems like sensible advice, and I can't really argue against it if you have the discipline to do it. But there is a better way in my experience. Paying off debt in order of the size of the loan gives folks the momentum they need to succeed at doing so. It provides those psychological wins to ensure they feel like progress is being made each time they check one off. Otherwise, they will get disheartened struggling all year just to clear one credit card. The short term goal is to reduce the number of loans; the long term goal is to reduce the overall balance.

Assets Vs Liabilities

In truth, this section very much relates to the notions of good and bad debt. However, there are some subtle differences which are why assets and liabilities require some consideration of their own. This section could also fall into either part of this book, I.e., the budgeting side or wealth growing/money allocation side as it incorporates a little of each. Hence why I have included it between them both.

Everybody has read or at least heard of the book *"Rich Dad, Poor Dad"* by Robert Kiyosaki. It's a personal finance classic and required reading for anyone trying to improve their financial health. The central theme of the book explores the notion of moving through the "cash flow quadrant" in order to create wealth, I.e., from an employee/self-employed person to a business owner/investor. But more importantly, Kiyosaki illustrates the benefits of increasing your exposure to cash flowing assets while eliminating the burden of money-losing liabilities. We touched on a few of these already, but I'll clarify them again here.

Anything which is producing you more money each month than it costs you to maintain. My favorites are now small businesses due to their scale-ability, but this can also include high yielding rental properties. But once more, a person's primary home can fall into either classification category, I.e., asset or liability. I'm not opposed to home ownership entirely. It's neutral to me. If you see yourself living there for the next 10-20 years, then you can ride out any downturn in the housing market and not have to sell. But don't use it as an ATM to continually withdraw equity to fund other purchases. Use it as a pension fund if anything. It's a long term play which you can call on later in life, not a short term investment.

Renting Vs Buying

This also very much comes down to your personal circumstance. What you are buying, how long are you going to use it for? What is the appreciation vs. depreciation likelihood? But also, how good is the finance you can secure on it? As a rule, buy anything you are going to get considerable use from, I.e., an exercise bike. Anything with minimal utility just rent, I.e., a chainsaw to trim the garden hedge once a year each summer. This seems obvious right? Shifting your habits to renting as opposed to buying is another excellent minimalist mindset to cultivate. I owned a set of DJ decks and mixer while I was in high school. I used them for a couple of weeks at most before discarding them to collect dust in the garage.

But again, the most prominent factor up for question in the renting vs. buying debate is a person's primary residence. If you have done your homework and have found a below market value property in a good location with excellent transport links, schools, and local amenities, then you're good. You have a high likelihood of price appreciation and a strong case for buying the place, especially if you plan to live there for at least the next decade. Just know that you will be putting down a hefty deposit more than likely. You have to assess whether that money could be better used elsewhere, such as a profitable cash flowing business. You will also have to deal with repairs and upkeep costs.

On the other hand, if you're renting a place, you forgo this significant outlay. Yes, it will cost you a little more in monthly payments depending on the size and location of the unit. But you will be free to move if your personal or professional situation changes. You will also be free of any tax and maintenance costs encumbered by the property, although these are often worked into rental rates anyway. This is typically an excellent option for younger working professionals in my opinion who don't want to get stuck in one particular place.

I know this all too well during my time traveling in Asia. In truth, there was very little chance I could have bought a place in any of the countries and cities I lived in. But I really got a feel for the benefits of living a semi-nomadic life within various minimalist apartments and the freedom this can bring. Now that I am back in the States, I have settled down somewhat and have switched to a buying mindset. It's horses for courses; you just have to figure out exactly what you want, and as always, know your numbers. What are the short, medium and long term implications of your choices and go from there.

PART 2: FILLING THE BUCKET

CHAPTER 4: GROWING WEALTH THE RIGHT WAY

"Don't tell me what your priorities are. Show me where you spend your money, and I'll tell you what they are"

(James Frick)

So now that we've looked at the most efficient ways to curb your spending, get your expenses in line, and budget wisely for what you have left. It's time for the more exciting stuff. Well, if you're like me, you find the saving strategies just as rewarding, but most people want a way to turbocharge their financial health once they've learned how to get in under control. I'm not talking about becoming reckless with your new found wealth. Just some suggestions that can help you get ahead. In reality, it's about becoming an intelligent distributor of the positive cash flow buffer we worked so hard to create in Part 1.

Again, we're not talking about rash risk-taking, just sensible money management. You will have to think about your finances in a different way, or your "Personal Economic Ecosystem" as I like to call it. But once you get used to this process, it will seem like second nature. You will also have to become comfortable with allocating some capital to various investment vehicles. But this also becomes easier the more you do it.

Creating such a system for myself has been the one thing that has helped me achieve finical freedom more than anything else I've tried. What I also know is that everything starts with what you are putting into the system. You can have the most well-oiled machine for growing your wealth, but if you have no money to feed into it, then nothing will happen. It's like owning a Ferrari but never filling it with gas. That is why you need to grasp the following concept before anything else.

Cash Flow Will Always Be King

There's a lot of debate over whether you should start a business or work your way up the corporate ladder these days. I find this to be somewhat redundant advice as its so specific to the individual and their current circumstance. What isn't in question is that you need to increase the amount of money you are bringing in each month to improve your financial status ultimately. Budgeting and saving can get you so far, but injecting more fuel into the engine is what really get things going. You don't have to be on the money making hamster wheel forever. But as a means to an end, we want to accelerate our way to the finish line for a few years, and that is done by adding cash flow.

Businesses typically fail not because they have poor ideas, products or processes. They fail because they do not have enough free working capital to sustain operations. They do not have enough money in the bank to make payroll each month. It's the same thing with our personal finances. If we can increase the amount of free liquid cash way have coming in, there's so much more we can do with it. But most importantly of all, it provides safety and stability. It's the lifeblood of the system.

This isn't a book on entrepreneurship or money making per se, but it's impossible to understand good money management and better budgeting without discussing the one factor which has the biggest impact of all. So how can we increase this income stream each month? For the majority of individuals, this will be going for that higher position at work to increase their salary. For others, it will be starting a side hustle, if not a full-time business of their own. Again, this is specific to the individual. Of course, there is greater scope for scaling within your own company, but there is also the risk of lost time and capital.

Whatever route you decide to take, upping your free cash flow is essential for making the next stage in the process work more efficiently. It certainly makes things more exciting for sure. By increasing top line income first, budgeting becomes that much easier, and as I say, the next set of the strategies will work more smoothly. You will have more wiggle room to play with and get yourself ahead that much faster. So now that we've decided that having a healthy and steady input into the system is crucial. We need to understand the other major principle of good money management.

What They Don't Teach You at School

The following is a relatively old concept in the personal finance and investment literature. There have been many books, articles, and studies written professing the benefits of paying yourself first. I think I first read about it in the excellent book by George Clason *"The Richest Man In Babylon."* But why is this practice considered so important? Why should you allocate money to yourself first from your salary and investments? Isn't all of it yours already? As we have seen in Part 1 of this book, when you budget correctly, much of your money will be squared away on bills and expenses leaving you very little, if any, at the end of the month. Most people are okay with this, they just accept it as a fact of life. This is the first major mindset shift you will have to make.

When you think about it, paying yourself first seems like a sensible strategy right? Yes and no. I'm not suggesting to go out and splurge on yourself the second you get paid. We are merely talking about siphoning a modest amount of your income, I.e., 10% to pay yourself first and foremost and no matter what else happens. Putting YOU at the front of the queue for perhaps the first time in your life. This is the beginning stage of building the foundations to the system.

Next, we will be discussing how to store and allocate the rest of your income, I.e., how much you should be saving, and how much you should be investing and where. But regardless of how you slice this pie, the one element which always stays the same is paying yourself a percentage of your monthly income first. Yes, that is before any rent or bills are paid or investments made. Period. This is for good reason. It's critical for your psychology more than anything. It produces the most significant shift in those who've never tried it before. So that being said, let's start to break down what these specific allocation models look like.

Traditional Allocation Rules

Most people have heard of the "Jam Jar Method." If you haven't, it goes something like this. Set up a bunch of physical containers (actual jars or pots), label each of them with the various outlays you need to make each month, I.e., taxes, bills, education, etc and place the correct amount of cash in each to pay them accordingly. This way everything is segregated nicely and never gets mixed up. I think it was merely an upgrade on the old piggy bank saving method originally, where your cash was stashed in one pot. When you think about it, having just one bank account to hold all of your money is pretty much the same thing. But this is far from optimal as I'll explain in a second. At the very least you should have a separate account in order to pay taxes each year.

So how does a savvy individual who has learned to arrange their own finances more prudently handle these allocations? There are many ways you can do it and the percentages can be adjusted somewhat to suit your current situation. But if you want the best results possible, I suggest sticking to what I'm about to recommend as closely as you can. This has not only worked wonders for me over the years but countless others I've shown it to also.

So what do these allocation figures look like? They are 10%, 40%, 50% which relates to savings, investments and living expenses respectively. I.e., Save 10% (pay yourself first), Invest 40% (at various risk levels) and necessities (food, rent, bills) for the remaining 50%. Yes, that's right, pay all of your regular outgoings with just 50% of your paycheck! Now you can see why I started with advice to up your incoming cash flow. This may seem like an impossible feat to some of you now, but bear with me a moment and let's go through the system to get a better idea of what we're talking about here.

Your Personal Economic Ecosystem
The 10%

Some people refer to this initial 10% as a rainy day fund. I suppose it's okay to view it that way if you see a rainy day as being some unforeseen medical emergency and the like. To say that either your life or that of a family member depended on it. Anything less is not acceptable. It's certainly not a pot to dip into every time your neighbor has a new hot stock pick to invest in, and definitely not for that holiday deal or new pair of shoes. This is where the mindset and psychological stuff really comes into play. You want to store this money away in a very secure and safe environment where you can't get to it easily.

This can be in a different account within the same bank, or a different one altogether. Regardless, it should be a highly inconvenient place to access. In essence, the polar opposite of most peoples standard checking accounts. You want no debit card, no cheque book, and no online banking facility. Virtually no way to make withdrawals other than driving over to the branch and getting the bank manager to write you out a cashiers cheque. You want to place as many hurdles between you and this money as possible. Ideally, a 2-3 hour drive if you can. Then, if you do ever have to make the trip, you should almost view it as stealing from yourself. I labeled it the "drive of shame" the one time I did have to make the trip. It's funny how your behavior and habits change once you correctly modify your thinking ahead of time.

Any bank will provide you with a low-interest savings account to get you started with this practice. You won't get rich off the measly 0.08% annual interest you'll gain. But it will be segregated which is the point. I'm not talking about 401(k)s or ISA's if you live in the UK. I still class these as low-risk investments (which we'll get onto next). It should be cash, with no exposure to money markets. The only risk to it is hyperinflation or the bank going under. Although we will have much bigger problems if either of these instances does occur. But that is a topic for a much longer book!

Some folks will say that it's stupid to leave any amount of money in a bank and not have it working for you. You can't argue with this on paper when looking at the pure maths. But in reality, the psychological benefits such as increased confidence and peace of mind are critical in the real world. Putting 10% of your income aside in savings works wonders for this. It's the first step in becoming financially free. Its the first test of good money discipline. It shifts the whole mindset from paying everyone else and hoping there's 10% left for you to take. To taking it first and leave everyone else vying for the rest!

The 40%

Now it's time for the real fun to start, and where you can get creative. This is the time to start making our money work was us. Ideally, we want the profits from these investments to pay for all of our outgoings and lifestyle eventually. But let's not get ahead of ourselves, for now, it's about making a start — a step into the investing world. I say investing, but this can be any additional money-making business — anything which is giving you a stable monthly return. The risk should also be staggered within the 40% as well.

I like to set mine up with 20% low risk (401(k)s/ISA's), 10% medium risk (Stable Index tracker funds), 5% high risk (Forex/Options Funds) and 5% education or "experimental" capital (taking courses, trying out new strategies, etc). Working out what this mini investment profile looks like to you will depend on your personal risk tolerance and your ability to identify good investments. But as a rule of thumb, always skew the majority of this portion to the lower risk vehicles, and less to the higher risk ones for obvious reasons. You stand a much lower chance of losing this principle capital by doing so. This is a long term game remember.

So it's now time for you to start investigating some of these strategies for yourself. I have just outlined some for you here. In reality, investing is a far bigger scope for a discussion on budgeting, but I wanted to give you a good idea of where to start when considering how to manage your money more efficiently. I'm not a financial adviser and do not know what options are available to you. I'm simply giving you an idea of how to start thinking about how to allocate your money a little more wisely. To help change your mindset to benefit your future self better.

The 50%

So this is what is left for you to spend. Your new disposable income! Sounds difficult right? Why is that? Again, it comes down to mindset and our basic financial literacy. Nobody taught us this stuff in school. We were all conditioned to live paycheck to paycheck from watching everyone around us. To leverage everything we made to attain the best house, car, and lifestyle we could "afford." But this is a terrible way to view the situation. If we all left high school or colleague with the mindset of living off 50%

of what we earned, we would be so much better off. We would find a way to make it work even if it meant living with parents for an extra couple of years.

I know what you're thinking "but I'm older and have much more responsibilities now, I can't live off just 50% of my salary and put the rest into savings and investments". But ask yourself this question instead "if I could find a way to make this work no matter how painful, to begin with, what would the rest of my life be like never having to worry about money again?" All of a sudden you would start getting very creative. You would be forced to make the adjustments and face up to some harsh decisions about your current lifestyle. Even if its simply canceling the cable subscription for a while, downsizing the car, or forgoing that summer vacation. Making some of these sacrifices now to get your personal finance machine working for you in the future is such a wise move to make.

I know things seem tight in today's economy, but again, I submit to you that with a little creative thinking and a big mental shift, you can start to head in this direction. If you need to bump up the 50% to 70% initially then so be it. But try to bring it down into the 50's once you get 6-12 months of proper budgeting experience behind you. This really is the sweet spot in terms of producing sustained money stability. It was for me anyway.

Up to this point, I couldn't work out why my monetary situation wasn't getting any better, even after I started to implement many of my other minimalist tendencies. Something was still missing. So I studied the finance and investment world to see where I was going wrong. To see how they allocated funds and grew existing businesses. I essentially reversed engineered some of their best practices and combined them with some existing personal finance strategies I knew, and voilà! Everything started to change. Money began accruing nicely within my various accounts, and I actually enjoyed logging into them each month to see how much they had increased.

This reality isn't out of reach for anyone. The only question is, will you now start making the changes required to produce these results in your life?

CHAPTER 5: GROWTH CURVES & MONEY PROJECTIONS

"A year from now you will wish you had started today"

(Karen Lamb)

In the previous chapter, I laid out the rudiments for your Personal Economic Ecosystem. For some, this will be their first foray into personal money management strategies. Hopefully, you should start to be seeing the power of putting these simple concepts into practice for yourself. If you are still somewhat skeptical or on the fence about trying them, I've included the following section to help convince you of their effectiveness. So let us discuss some of the major principles which underpin these tactics. The natural laws which drive wealth growth to see if I can persuade you to give them a shot.

Parkinson's Law

The first of these natural tendencies was described by Cyril Parkinson, a British naval historian, and author in the 1950's. Parkinson explained how virtually everything in life would expand to fill its boundaries. Gas will naturally fill a container, people will stretch out work to fill the time within an allotted deadline, and bureaucracies will grow with the size of an organization. This law very much applies to our finances too.

You will naturally spend what you have if you don't put measures into place to manage your money better. If I put a cookie in front of you, you'll probably eat it. If I put ten cookies in front of you, you'll almost certainly eat more than one, probably several if you're anything like me… This is Parkinson's Law at work. With the availability of abundant funds, we will consume those resources in a much more liberal fashion. If funds are scarce, however, we do the opposite. We become imaginative and resourceful. It typically takes the same amount of time to go through the first 90% of the toothpaste as it does to use up the last 10%. OK, that might be a slight exaggeration, but you get what I mean. We suddenly start to use it very sparingly and get much better at squeezing and turning the tube to get at every last bit.

It's the same with money, if you're not setting up measures to manage it wisely, it will disappear on all sorts of stuff. If however, you place restrictions on yourself via proper budgeting and allocation of those funds, you start to function much more frugally. You are forced to find ways to increase your income and see where you can squeeze the most out of an existing business. It pushes you to work harder and ask for that raise, to improve your skills to become more valuable to the market place. It enables you to expand into the person you need to be in order to grow.

Setting up a proper money management system promotes this in every way. It allows us to rise above the feast and famine mentality that almost every human being goes through on this planet. In reality, it doesn't matter what percentages you settle on precisely. As long as you pick a strategy and stick to it! Consistency is the key. Nothing works unless you allow it enough time to do its thing. Which brings us nicely onto the next topic.

Compounding Interest

Albert Einstein described this force as the 8th wonder of the world. He was, of course, referring more specifically to observations within the universe, to galaxy and individual planet formations. Compounding demonstrates the quickening growth rates of objects when additional mass is added. As we will see shortly, humans are typically very bad at thinking in probabilities, and this especially applies to projecting and calculating these future growth curves.

Everyone has heard of the doubling penny conundrum. If you haven't, it goes something like this. If I gave you a choice between $200,000 in cash now, or the amount of money from doubling a penny each day for the next 30 days, which would you choose? Almost everyone initially opts for the $200,000 in your hand. But once you look at the numbers in the second scenario, you realize that you made a big mistake. If you had held out for the penny to double each day for a month, you would have received over five million dollars instead.

There's a couple of important points to note here. Firstly, that our linear thinking brains were widely out of whack with reality. A penny doubling for 30 days far exceeded our expectations. But more importantly than this, we have almost no real comprehension for how and when these more substantial gains were accumulated, I.e., towards the back end of the doubling cycle. If you were watching the sequence for the entire time, you would see that the total is still only at $163 at the halfway point (15 doubles).

Therefore, it takes consistency and time to realize this compounding effect. In fact, when you look at the initial growth rate of such a system, it seems almost flat-lined and negligible, to begin with. But this is what trips most people up. They feel the pain of proper budgeting and money management when they first attempt it, but can't see any significant returns. They become discouraged and blow all of their cash without ever actualizing the magic which occurs only 2-3 years down the road. All they had to do was stick to the prudent path instead.

Pareto Principle

I've talked about the basic concepts of the 80/20 rule within *"Minimalist Living"* when it comes to productivity and tasks. In truth, it's a much broader concept than most people give it credit for. It was derived from the Pareto Principle which was initially described by Italian economist Vilfredo Pareto in the late 1800s. To summarize this law for those who aren't sure what I'm referring to, the 80/20 rule simply states that when you look at a large number of occurrences, roughly 80% of the results will come from 20% of the actions. It's the reason why you should assess what you're good at, the things which produce you most of your results and focus on only doing them.

However, there is an extension to this concept called the "Power Law" or "Pareto Distribution" which explains the inherent wealth and resource distribution (and more importantly the disparities) within all observable phenomena. Social groups, economies, and biological ecosystems all display this type of distribution pattern, I.e., where 80% of the wealth gravitates towards 20% of the population averagely speaking. Of course, there are gradations within this general pattern especially when you get to the extremes, like the top and bottom 1%. Whether you view this as being the result of diligent hard work, competence levels, intellect or some sort of oppressive force is beside the point. There's no question that the Pareto Principle permeates all systems and forms of life across the board. Once again, our finances are no exception to this.

What I find the most interesting about the concept is seeing how it plays out at certain junctures in the model. More specifically what seems to happen when you get close to the top or bottom 20% level. At this point, progress starts to quicken in either direction exponentially. It explains why negative spirals can get out of hand so quickly. If you come into work drunk, you might get fired. If you decide to improve your habits and find another job, then you can arrest the slide and start moving back up the success scale. If however, you continue to drink excessively, not find another job, you may well end up losing your house and friends to boot! At some point (around the bottom 20% tipping point) its like falling off a cliff.

But the same applies to the opposite end of the spectrum. If you are diligently and consistently working hard towards worthy aims and goals, at some point I.e. near the top 20% level, your opportunities start to come in at an ever-increasing rate. You begin to get bigger and better job offers and requests for collaboration with others almost to the point that you can't handle anymore. At this point, it seems unfair to the outsider looking in. You are viewed as "lucky" when this couldn't be further from the truth.

You see this all the time with products in the marketplace. If you take the three most established vacuum cleaners, for instance. There may only be a slight difference in quality between the 3, but that doesn't play out in sales numbers. People assume that the distribution will be linear with the top product receiving around 50% of sales, the next best getting 35%, and the third best perhaps 15%. But that is not the case. The top perceived products will typically garner over 90% of total sales, the second best will get around 10%, while the third being lucky to receive 1%. This pattern replicates itself in almost every market or industry. Just look at the stats for the top content providers on YouTube for instance. They receive the vast majority of views, and subsequent ad revenue while all of the smaller channels complain about how unfair it is.

So the trick is to start allowing this concept to work in your own life. To test and try enough low, medium and high-risk investment vehicles to see which is producing the best return. Remember that at some point this 80/20 rule will start to become clear. One income avenue will begin to grow head and shoulders above the others, allowing you to focus on it much more. But you have to be willing to experiment and as always, give things time to play out. If you can, you will find yourself gravitating towards to top 20% in no time.

So there you have it. Three power principles to help us more clearly understand our money management activities. Other than being very cool concepts to be aware of. They highlight some of the natural laws which govern pretty much everything, not least when it comes to growing our wealth. If you can understand these principles and get them working in your favor, as opposed to against you, that is half of the battle. They naturally take over and do the heavy lifting before long. Your money starts to compound and grow faster and faster almost on autopilot. But you need the discipline to stick with it and adjust your time horizons for results. If you need some extra help with this, the following chapter will show you how.

CHAPTER 6: DELAYING GRATIFICATION

"Every time you borrow money, you're robbing your future self"

(Nathan Morris)

Short Term Goals = Long Term Payoffs

We've touched on goals for clearing your debts. But what do you do once you're back in the black? You need some metrics to track growth as well. Much of this has to do with personal psychology as always. You need some short term targets to aim for which will be your monthly goals. For this, I suggest setting up a tracking sheet. Mint.com can also help you with this although nothing is wrong with a good ole excel spreadsheet either.

I can't stress enough the importance of putting short term budgeting, saving and allocation metrics and mechanisms into place in order to meet these goals. You really need to "fall in love with the process, and the results will take care of themselves." We've already seen how the compounding effect and Pareto Distribution will take care of the rest if you stay the course. I appreciate it's difficult to do in practice due to our ingrained behaviors. If you are still struggling with this, it might also be for the following reason.

Thinking in Probabilities

Humans are typically very bad at assessing probabilities. It's not just that very few of us like dealing with numbers, and even fewer are good with them. It's that our brains aren't primed for making these calculations very well. Even though we have developed the complex reasoning centers of the neocortex which allows for language, spatial reasoning, and sensory perception, we still have a tough time judging risk. These newer upgrades to the wetwear in our heads often get tangled up with the older and more primitive regions of the limbic system such as the amygdala. One is attempting to think its way out of a problem, while the other is invoking a "fight or flight" response within us. Unfortunately, these older centers of the mammalian brain often win the day, as we haven't yet caught up to the civilized and technological world we now inhabit. It was much more important to make a quick escape from the jaws of a saber-toothed tiger who potentially lurked in the bushes than it was to try and over analyze our way out of the problem.

So we act rashly "in the moment" as we can't connect the dots very well into the future. This leads us to significantly overestimate what we can do in the near term, I.e., one year, but highly underestimate what we can do in ten years. Our linear thinking systems can't compute exponential growth. Progress is viewed as a steady state increase, in terms of a fixed percentage, I.e., 20% per year. However, in reality, things do not play out like this in the real world. In this sense, humans are terrible long term forecasters. We are essentially akin to fortune tellers when we attempt to do this.

This is why you need a system to put into place for the monthly planning strategies similar to the ones I'm suggesting in the book. Habits that heavily stack the probabilities in your favor in the long run. Focus on the short term goals and the exponential compound effect will take care of future growth. Thinking in these mechanical terms mean we eliminate much of the emotional baggage attributed to our money mindset. We alleviate any compulsive behavior while reducing fear and anxiety at the same time.

Most people view their financial life as a slot machine. They put quarters in hoping for a random positive result. If you play long enough, you're bound to hit the jackpot at some point right? Not the case my friend. The lottery is an excellent example of this; it's such a bad trade-off in terms of probabilities. But most people view it as such a small outlay they might as well have a punt. But in reality, this is just another tax on the masses when you do the math.

In truth, it takes a predetermined set of strategies which stack the odds in your favor. It's like designing a game you know you can win. That is precisely what setting up your personal money management, and budgeting system provides. If you do A, you get B over time. Not betting the farm on any one project or investment, and certainly not blowing your budget on conspicuous consumption each month. But when done correctly, it takes luck out of the equation. Much of this has to do with delaying gratification, which we'll get onto now.

Marshmallows & Money

Developing overall self-discipline is one of the most critical attributes to achieving success in any area of life. It's the one thing I notice that makes the most significant difference within people who are attempting to manage their money better. Taking on a life of minimalism has undoubtedly helped me cultivate this ability over the years, although I know it's a character trait which is in short supply in much of society today.

But having a high degree of self-regulation is critical to making your budgeting plans play out the way you want them to. Having the ability to suppress the need for instant gratification can go a long way in terms of creating long term and sustainable wealth. Gratification refers merely to a reward or satisfaction we receive, typically in return for some work performed on our part. It's much healthier for our mindset when this reward is granted for effort, especially if there is a delayed response or waiting time between the two. Usually the longer you can stretch this payoff period the better.

But again, we are fighting very ingrained evolutionary impulses here. We have been hardwired to eat the food we gathered today, and procreate without delay as tomorrow was never promised.

I know that nothing is a given in our current day and age, but the probabilities suggest we are much more likely to survive the winter in our centrally heated homes I can assure you. It's now far wiser to prevent short-term self-sabotaging behavior in the 21st century. To forgo smaller and more immediate rewards like buying those shoes, as you will reap much bigger and better ones (like full financial freedom) at some point in the future.

Stanford Marshmallow Experiment

Most folks have come across this study at some point, as it's equally compelling as it is revealing. The Stanford marshmallow experiment was conducted in the 1960s and 1970s by psychologist Walter Mischel, who was a professor at Stanford University at the time. The basic premise of these experiments was simply to test what would happen when a set of children were given the option of receiving a small reward immediately, I.e., 1 marshmallow, or a larger reward, I.e., 2 marshmallows, if they could wait out a fifteen minute time period. At this point, the experimenter would leave the participant by themselves with the treat to contemplate what they wanted to do, the ultimate test of self-control to your average five-year-old.

So what did they find? The majority of the kids gobbled up the marshmallow without delay; a number held out for a few minutes before also succumbing to the temptation. But a handful managed to sit quietly for the entire fifteen minutes after which they were indeed rewarded with a second marshmallow. However, the most intriguing findings from this study weren't these initial observations of self-restraint. They came from the follow-up research conducted on the same participants at later stages in their lives.

Those who waited out the fifteen minutes in the original test, I.e., could delay their instant gratification, scored better in every other marker of success such as SAT scores, physical health, and economic achievements. While the study does suggest that there is a substantial genetic component with regards to self-discipline (as signified by the results of the initial research while the participants were still very young). Not all hope is lost for us avid marshmallow consumers. It just means that we have to recognize this trait within us and intentionally cultivate the qualities which are more likely to bring us long term success. Simply following the budgeting and planning rules highlighted in the book is a great place to start!

SUMMARY: SAVING DOLLARS, MAKING CENTS...

"You must gain control over your money or the lack of it will forever control you"

(Dave Ramsey)

Core Concepts Summary

If I were to boil down my best advice into a nutshell, it would be this. Reduce your spending, make more money, and don't upgrade your lifestyle in lock step with your improved financial status. Not rocket science I think you'll agree. It's typically very difficult to downgrade once you have achieved a certain level of material things. The fear of lack of social proof we are signaling to others is just too high. It can often take a switch to outright minimalism to justify the change in your mind.

"The art of living easily as to money is to pitch your scale of living one degree below your means" as English poet Henry Taylor once stated. I actually think you should aim for a wider margin between the two to really create that positive cash flow buffer which is so important to getting ahead. A kind of "The Millionaire Next Door" scenario described in Thomas Stanley's and William Danko's book of the same name.

But if I were to distill the best practices laid out in this book into simple and actionable steps, they would be the following:

1) Get rid of bad debt and liabilities & acquire paying assets instead.

2) Never let your primary income die & increase it at every opportunity.

3) Allocate these funds accordingly within the saving and investing guidelines set out in your personal money management system.

4) Continue performing the above steps until the passive income from your investments matches or exceeds your primary income (I.e. true financial freedom)

At this point, everything should be running like a well-oiled machine, and you will reach your savings and money goals by default. It makes no difference where you're from, your background or what level you are starting at. What matters is that you start. That you implement the methods in your own life right away. It has a 100% success rate for those who stick with it for the long term. It's impossible not to, as its simple math. It's fear and momentary lack of control leading to compulsive spending which trips people up. For this, I have one last piece of advice to help you nail your psychology once and for all.

A Crisis is Always in the Making

Even though I've massively cut down my digital and internet use over the past few years, it still seems impossible to go more than a few minutes without being subjected to some news suggesting an impending market crash. Money blogs, financial newsletters and investment YouTube channels alike… The doomsdayers are everywhere. I'm not implying there is no validity whatsoever to these claims. I certainly felt the pain back in 2008. But that was because I was financed to the max. If you follow the steps in this book to simplify your spending, improve your budgeting skills and incorporate your Personal Economic Ecosystem for allocating and growing wealth, then you'll be just fine as the system should scale to meet any markets condition. It will scale up in a good economy and down a in a bad one.

So, in my opinion, it's a good idea to ignore these clever clickbait tactics which only ensure more eyeballs on their articles. They are simply copying what mainstream media has been doing for decades. As we have already discussed, we humans are evolutionarily hardwired to zero in on danger, and these content creators are all too aware of this. It's officially known as the "Negativity Bias" to psychologists. It explains why we inherently focus in on unpleasant outcomes. The old printing press adage that "If it bleeds it leads," couldn't be more accurate.

Even though much of this scaremongering might be pointless pessimism, the markets do definitely crash from time-to-time, so we can't dismiss these warning signs entirely. In fact, as history shows us, there is a significant market correction every 8-10 years or so. This is especially relevant at the moment of writing, as we are entering new territory within the financial markets, I.e., We are now experiencing the longest bull run in recorded history (3,453 days or 9.5 years).

In other words, we are due for a correction. So the question remains, what should we be doing in the face of this inevitable downturn? The short answer to this is simple. Nothing. Presuming you have made and are continuing to make prudent moves with your money, then carry on as usual. It's no secret that I prefer income producing assets and investment funds to feed into my monthly positive cash flow — things like rental properties, and historically stable dividend producing blue-chip stocks such as AT&T or BP.

When experiencing a mild recessionary correction or even a full-on 40%-50% crash, you just do the same thing. You continue investing into these asset classes at the now discounted prices in a dollar cost averaging fashion. Yes, you may take a short term paper loss on the list/stock price, but who cares? You are still getting paid the dividends to wait it out. You may have to stomach a slight reduction in rentals yields on property for instance, but that will be the worst of it.

This is why I have focused the second part to this book on the psychological principles of sound money management, as they are just as important, if not more so than the technical aspects of budgeting and allocation. Understanding why we behave the way we do so you can downplay these tendencies ahead of time. To provide you with the factors which really matter when it comes to our financial stability and money growth. Principles such as compounding interest, Pareto Distribution curves, and Parkinson's Law. If you can put these factors in your favor, you'll be just fine.

CONCLUSION

"The saving man becomes the free man."

(Chinese Proverb)

It's often stated that humans are either running towards things they want or away from things they don't want. In other words, we are either seeking pleasure or avoiding pain in a psychological sense. In my experience, its usually the latter. But even when we indulge in acts of instant gratification, this paradoxically provides our future selves more pain by doing so. That is why budgeting and growing your money correctly is such a wise choice to make. It gets us out of the pleasure and pain cycle and allows us to fulfill our ultimate goal, which is to be free (at least in a financial sense) which is the same thing for most people.

Notice that I didn't say happy. That is derived from other places. But it does make you comfortable. Therefore, taking control of your financial future is possibly the most important thing you can do. It will have such wide-reaching ramifications on the rest of your life. It provides the peace of mind to enjoy your daily activities and those who you choose to spend it with. Proper budgeting and wealth growing strategies are a minimalists dream. Because, let's face it, even when cutting down the number of things you own, you still have to function in societies economy which is money based whether we like it or not. Of course, you can go "off grid" and live in a wood cabin in the forest. But this isn't necessary yet if you can be disciplined with yourself for a few years.

You don't need millions in the bank to make this work. You don't need to earn tens of thousands of dollars a month either. You just have to learn the fundamentals of good personal money management and apply them strictly over enough time. It's not the sexiest advice which I warned you at the beginning of this book, but it works. I wouldn't be telling you otherwise. It's freed me and now my small family in such a liberating way, it's too valuable not to share. The only question is, will you now take control of your own financial destiny. Whether you are a practicing minimalist or not, makes no difference. Learning how to budget like one is a sage move to make. Being free of monetary worries is a gift like no other, and hopefully, I've provided you with some help in getting you one step closer to this wonderful goal.

Take Care

Jason

P.s. I just want to thank you for purchasing this book personally. If you happened to enjoy the content than I'd love to hear your feedback. I would very much appreciate if you could leave a review after reading. Comments on how these concepts may have helped you are both interesting for me to read, as well as aiding others in finding this information!

BONUS CHAPTER

(From "Minimalist Living")

CHAPTER 6: TRANSPORTATION & TRAVEL

"Minimalism is asking why before you buy."

(Francine Jay)

Transit Tips

I mentioned my beloved BMW 5 series within the introduction to this book. I really enjoyed driving that car, but in reality, it was overkill in terms of space, horsepower, and gas-guzzling ability. It had too much of these things if truth be told. In essence, it cost me far more compared with the payoff it was providing. Many of us fall into this trap while attempting to keep up with the Joneses. I'm not trying to be a killjoy here. Many of you (especially the guys) may have a liking for exotic and fast cars. If this is your thing, then, by all means, get the one you want for a while. But the fact remains, you only really enjoy these things for a while. I want an Aston Martin, but I know I will sell it within a year or two when my young family comes along, as it will just not be practical anymore.

Like everything with this mindset, it's about cutting down to simplify your life. Many believe that it requires selling all of your vehicles and opting for public transport instead. There is some logic behind this. I mean, do you really own your car anyway? Or does it own you? I'm the one who has to service it each year. I'm the one who has to fill it with gas, change the oil and pay for its storage wherever I go. But it just comes down to your personal circumstance. If getting the train, bus, or better yet, cycling to the office works for you, then do it. You will be cutting down your carbon footprint and perhaps getting in shape if you can manage this. But don't make things considerably more painful for yourself if driving the family sedan does the job just fine.

Its really about performing a cost analysis as well as a convenience check. Work out exactly how much your vehicle is costing you in finance and upkeep. The American Automobile Association frequently surveys car owners and found that the average person outlays around $8,5000 per year by owning one. That works out to roughly $700 per month when insurance, taxes, repairs and parking fees are factored in. Again, I'm not saying do away with your vehicle without delay, just clearly understand what it's costing you and where you can make some savings. Can you downsize and pocket yourself some cash? Can you sell your car and make do with using ride-sharing apps such as Uber? For some folks, they can't do away with this mode of transportation entirely for understandable and logistical reasons, and that's just fine. Only you know your current circumstance, just ensure you know your numbers before making any decisions.

Even if you do decide to keep the four wheels. You can always cut down the need to drive it everywhere. I mean, do you really need to drive a mile and a half to the store each day? Or can you take a walk or cycle instead? It's simply a value calculation as always regarding the monetary cost, time efficiency as well as your health. Only once all of these considerations are factored in can you make these decisions wisely. Gone are the days when communities used to help one another out by carpooling to work, or taking turns to taxi kids to and from school. If you're fortunate enough to still enjoy this environment where you live, then make full use of it.

Vacation Considerations

Minimalism is widely considered the practice of tidying up your home and living space. But one of the biggest benefits of clearing out the unneeded clutter from your life is that it allows you to travel more freely, more often, and much lighter when you do. You can save on expensive luggage allowances, take advantage of last minute cheap flight tickets. But most importantly of all, frees you in a psychological sense to enjoy your destination that much more. You can take in the sights and surroundings without the constant need to plan for the logistics of carting around your stuff!

Traveling naturally forces us to return to a minimalist state. You pack your things, grab your passport and head out the door. Yes you might feel that nagging sense that you've forgotten something, but you know it will only be a peripheral item, you have the essentials. You rock up at your hotel room where everything is tidy, and all you need is immaculately laid out for you. These instances are a true minimalist sanctuary for the time being. You are free to put down your stuff and go and explore the city you've found yourself in. However, it can be done incorrectly if you are not careful.

I remember being in Koh Phangan, Thailand some years ago. The island which made full moon parties popular. It's very much a beaten track tourist spot these days, although most young Westerners still travel quite light when they go. But I'll never forget seeing a group of young American girls struggling to haul their ginormous pink suitcases off the long-tail boats, which ferried people to the beach drop off points. I recall thinking to myself "whatever you have in that monstrosity, must really be worth it". In reality, it was almost certainly an abundance of clothes, hairdryers and other pointless accessories unsuited to the humid South-East Asian climate.

So how do you avoid this pitfall yourself? The first thing to do in my opinion begins with getting your packing game right. It all starts from here, and with a little planning as always. Getting yourself one well-organized travel bag is such a wise investment to make. Something medium-sized and durable, which can go in both check-in luggage, or fit into the overhead compartments as a carry on bag. You only need enough space for a selective amount of essential clothes. This number will obviously depend on the length of your trip. It's a good idea to plan for laundry too, in order to cut down the need for excessive garments anyway. I'm a professional at finding local laundry places now, although most hotels will offer this service for a small fee too.

MINIMALIST BUDGET

Just pack for what is probable. Get out of the mindset of packing for all possibilities. Getting caught with your pants down in these situations rarely happens. It's not worth planning for it all your life, to satisfy the one time it does happen. There's good fun to be had being able to think on your feet when you need to become resourceful. This concept scares most people, but really, what's the worst that can happen anyway? You have to buy a cheap raincoat that you'll throw away after your trip. Its better than lugging around your heavy and expensive winter jacket everywhere you go "just in case."

Suitcase pockets are always desirable to store your selected items like electronics and toiletries. This is where you can make a significant impact on your minimalist traveling game. Most retail pharmacy stores and supermarkets stock small sized toiletries, I.e., under 100 milliliters, to not only save on space but ensure you pass through security and costumes checks just fine. I've lost countless bottles of shampoo and shaving creams due to the crazy fluids and liquid restrictions of airlines. If you often travel (like me), you can take full advantage of the miniature shampoos and shower gels most hotels will provide. Just take a couple when you leave and fill them up with your own toiletries when you next fly.

With a little planning and foresight, you can make traveling a genuinely enjoyable and stress-free experience again, which its always supposed to have been. You just have to learn to let go and relax. Some of the best times I've spent away are resolving minor mishaps. I never allow room for anything drastic to happen, especially on business trips. But vacations are your time to be free of the worries that even your everyday minimalism lifestyle provides. Travel broadens the mind, so don't deteriorate the experience by worrying about unnecessary stuff. That completely defeats the point of this philosophy entirely!

www.ingramcontent.com/pod-product-compliance
Lightning Source LLC
Chambersburg PA
CBHW072015230526
45468CB00021B/1570